# SHARE A STORY
# The
# Ravenous Beast

# Introduction

One of the best ways you can help
your children learn and learn to read
is to share books with them. Here's why:

• They get to know the **sounds**, **rhythms** and **words**
used in the way we write. This is different from how we
talk, so hearing stories helps children learn how to read.

• They think about the **feelings** of the characters
in the book. This helps them as they go about
their own lives with other people.

• They think about the **ideas** in the book. This helps
them to understand the world.

• Sharing books and listening to what your children
say about them shows your children that you care
about them, you care about what they think
and who they are.

*Michael Rosen*

Michael Rosen
*Writer and Poet*
*Children's Laureate (2007-9)*

For Megan

First published 2003 by Walker Books Ltd
87 Vauxhall Walk, London SE11 5HJ

This edition published 2011

2 4 6 8 10 9 7 5 3 1

© 2003 Niamh Sharkey
Concluding notes © CLPE 2011

Printed in China

British Library Cataloguing in Publication Data:
a catalogue record for this book is available from the British Library

ISBN 978-1-4063-3515-6

www.walker.co.uk

# The Ravenous Beast

## Niamh Sharkey

**WALKER BOOKS**
AND SUBSIDIARIES
LONDON • BOSTON • SYDNEY • AUCKLAND

"I AM
THE HUNGRIEST
ANIMAL OF ALL,"
said the Ravenous Beast.
"I'm hungry, hungry, hungry!
I'm so hungry I could eat
the big yellow house on the hill.
Gobble it up! Swallow it down!
Now THAT'S what I call hungry!"

"Nonsense! Smonsense!"

said the little white mouse. "No one's hungrier than me. I'm so hungry I could eat

a red boat and a ringing bell.

Nibble nibble! Tuck 'em away!

Now THAT'S what I call hungry!"

# "Hokum! Pokum!"

said the marmalade cat.
"I'm as hungry as can be.
I'm so hungry I could eat

a bucket, a spade and some red lemonade.

Gnaw 'em! Gulp 'em! Stuff 'em down!

Now THAT'S what
I call hungry!"

"Hooey!
Phooey!"

said the spotty dog.
"No one's hungrier than me.
I'm so hungry I could eat

a roller skate, a birthday cake,
a rubber duck, a ticking clock.

Slurp 'em! Burp 'em! Woof 'em down!

Now THAT'S what
I call hungry!"

# "Moo! Moo! Malarkey!"

said the black-and-white cow.
"I'm as hungry as can be.
I'm so hungry I could eat

a castle, a crown, the Queen's dressing-gown,
a wellie-boot, all the King's loot.

Munch 'em up! Crunch 'em down!

Now THAT'S what I call hungry!"

"Balderdash!
Baloney!"

said the green crocodile.
"No one's hungrier than me.
I'm so hungry I could eat

a suitcase, a wand, a Jack-in-the-box,

a polka-dot sock, a top hat and a spinning top.

Snip 'em up! Snap 'em down!

Now THAT'S what I call

hungry!"

"Flip! Flap-doodle!"
said the grinning lion.
"I'm as hungry as can be.
I'm so hungry I could eat

a ray gun, a rocket,
a humbug from my pocket,
a trampoline, a trombone with a dent,
a bouncing ball, a circus tent.

Bite 'em up! Bolt 'em down!
Now THAT'S
what I call
hungry!"

"Not on your nelly!"
said the big-eared elephant.
"No one's hungrier than me.
I'm so hungry I could eat

an aeroplane, a parachute,
a pot of tea, a hot-air balloon,
a tin of beans, a parcel, a kite and a green bus.

Suck 'em up! Scoff 'em down!

Now THAT'S what
I call hungry!"

## "Whoosh! Swoosh!"

said the gigantic whale.
"I'm as hungry as can be.
I'm so hungry I could eat

a pirate's ship, a treasure map,
a piggy bank, a yellow mac, an anchor, a chain,
a flag, a tin drum, yo-ho-ho and a barrel of rum.

Squish 'em in! Squash 'em down!

Now THAT'S what I
call hungry!"

# "STOP!"

said the Ravenous Beast.

"I AM the HUNGRIEST of all!

# I'm so hungry I'm going to eat

a little
white mouse

a marmalade
cat

a spotty
dog

a black-and-white
cow

a green
crocodile

a grinning
lion

a big-eared
elephant

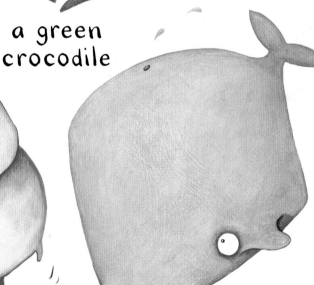

and a
gigantic whale."

"GOBBLE
YOU
UP!

SWALLOW
YOU
DOWN!"

# Sharing Stories

Sharing stories together is a pleasurable way
to help children learn to read and enjoy books.
Reading stories aloud and encouraging
children to talk about the pictures and join in
with parts of the story they know well are
good ways to build their interest in books.
They will want to share their favourite books
again and again. This is an important part
of becoming a successful reader.

**The Ravenous Beast** is a hungry beast, but is it the hungriest animal of all? The repetition, rhyme and quirky illustrations make this book a memorable reading adventure. Here are some ways you can share this book:

- This lively tale invites you to read it with lots of expression and different voices. Reading it aloud expressively is a great way to excite children about the story and to help them to read it for themselves.

- Invite them to join in with the repeated phrases. As they join in they can follow the words on the page.

- Children could add their own character to the list of hungry animals and say what it could eat. They can draw a picture to show this and you can help them add their ideas as a caption.

- Children can use the pictures to tell the story in their own words and speak in different voices to suit each character.

- Looking at the illustration of all the animals towards the end of the book, see if children can remember the characters in sequence. They can be the Ravenous Beast saying, "I'm so hungry I could eat a…" followed by the eight characters, if possible in order. If they can remember the descriptions, even better!

- What are the different ways of describing "eat"? Go through the book together and make a list, e.g. gobble, swallow, nibble, crunch.

- What do children think about the ending? Talk together about how the Ravenous Beast might feel.

# SHARE A STORY
## A First Reading Programme
### From Pre-school to School

Beginnings – 2 years+

Early Steps – 3 years+

Next Steps – 4 years+

Taking Off – 5 years+

# Sharing the best books makes the best readers

**WALKER BOOKS**

www.walker.co.uk